FOREST BOOKS
A VANISHING EMPTINESS

Born in Brussels in 1935, the Flemish writer WILLEM M. ROGGEMAN has made a name for himself as poet, novelist, and literary and artistic journalist. He has received a number of literary prizes and was lately decorated by the Belgian government when he was awarded the prestigious Order of Leopold II. At present he is living in the Netherlands, where he works as assistant director of the Flemish Cultural Centre in Amsterdam. Beginning with a poetry of verbal experiment, he soon graduated to a more accessible modernism, characterised in particular by its verbal ease and liveliness. He has been translated into a number of languages but this selection is the fullest and most comprehensive to date. The editor, YANN LOVELOCK, has counterpointed the contrasting manners in which Roggeman has written with the voices of a number skilful translators, and contributed an informative essay on the poet's work and development. Roggeman has often worked closely with artists who have illustrated his work. The illustrations and cover painting for this book are by the Belgian Pop artist Pol Mara.

POL MARA was born in Antwerp in December 1920 and now figures among the small number of Flemish painters who during their lifetime have gained an international reputation. He commenced his studies at the Antwerp Academy, later attending the Institut supérieur des beaux-arts. His first exhibition was held at Antwerp's Iris Gallery in 1952, and by 1962 he was regarded highly for his Pop Art style. During this year an exhibition of his work, 'Twelve Years of Pol Mara', was held at the Mickelson Gallery in Washington. Since then he has been awarded many prizes and in 1982 was commissioned for a monumental picture to decorate a wall at the Hebrew University in Jerusalem.

A
VANISHING
EMPTINESS

Willem's wings

A
VANISHING
EMPTINESS

Selected Poems
of
WILLEM M. ROGGEMAN

translated from the Dutch

Edited by
YANN LOVELOCK

FOREST BOOKS
LONDON ☆ 1989 ☆ BOSTON

PUBLISHED BY
FOREST BOOKS
20 Forest View, Chingford, London E4 7AY, U.K.
P.O. Box 438, Wayland, MA 01788, U.S.A.

First published 1989

Typeset in Great Britain by Cover to Cover, Cambridge
Printed in Great Britain by A. Wheaton & Co Ltd, Exeter

ISBN 0 948259 51 5

British Library Cataloguing in Publication Data:
A vanishing emptiness: selected poems of
Willem M. Roggeman
I. Title   II. Lovelock, Yann
839.3'2164

Library of Congress Catalogue Card No: 88–8259

Forest Books gratefully acknowledge the financial assistance of the
Foundation for Translations, Amsterdam and the Flemish Ministry of
Culture, Brussels.

The Translators

THEO HERMANS: b.1948 in Assent, Belgium. After studying at the universities of Ghent, Essex and Warwick, then teaching English at the University of Algiers, he now teaches Dutch at the University of London. He translates from English and Spanish into Dutch, besides from Dutch into English. Editor and part-translator of Hugo Claus' *Selected Poems 1953–73* (Aquila, 1986) and part of the team who translated Claus' *The Sign of the Hamster* (Louvain, 1986). He has been one of the editors of *Dutch Crossing*: a journal of Low Countries Studies, since 1977.

DOROTHY HOWARD: born and educated in Toronto, Canada. Author of two books of poems and one of verse for children. Former director of the Windsor chapter of the Canadian Authors Association and a member of the Canadian Association for the Advancement of Netherlandic Studies. Together with Hendrika Ruger she has also published an anthology of Dutch poetry, *Under Dutch Skies* (Netherlandic Press, 1981).

YANN LOVELOCK: b.Birmingham, 1939 and educated at Oxford and Sheffield universities. Author of several collections of poetry and experimental prose. Co-ordinator of Angulimala, the Buddhist Prison Chaplaincy Organisation. Translator and editor of an anthology of Belgian poetry in the Walloon dialect, *The Colour of the Weather* (Menard Press, 1980) and author of a study of modern Dutch poetry in English translation, *The Line Forward* (Bridges Books, Amsterdam, 1984).

PETER NIJMEIJER: b.1947 in Amsterdam, Netherlands. A poet in his own right as well as translator and promotor of Dutch poetry, he is also a prolific translator of English-language poetry into Dutch. During a prolonged stay in England during the '70s he was responsible for several publications together with Paul Brown of Transgravity Press, most notably *4 Dutch Poets, 4 Flemish Poets*, Hans Verhagen's *Stars over Bombay* (all 1976), and Sybren Polet's *X-Man* (1979). Soon after his return he worked for a while in the Foundation for Translations in Amsterdam. At present he is living near Naas in Ireland.

Hendrika Ruger: b.1928 in Utrecht, Netherlands. Emigrated to Canada in 1951 and has lived since in Windsor, Ontario. Educated at the universities of Windsor and Utrecht. A founding member of the Windsor chapter of the Canadian Association for the Advancement of Netherlandic Studies and a contributor to the *Canadian Journal of Netherlandic Studies*. Besides working with Dorothy Howard on the anthology *Under Dutch Skies*, she was one of the team responsible for the Netherlandic Press' anthology of contemporary women writers in Dutch, *With Other Words* (1985) and edited its anthology of Dutch-Canadian writing, *From a Chosen Land* (1986).

Acknowledgements

My thanks are due to the other translators who have allowed me to use their work in this selection, and to the publishers and editors of anthologies and magazines in which much of this material first appeared. The poems translated by Dorothy Howard and Hendrika Ruger appeared in their dual-language selection of Roggeman's poems, *The Revolution Begins in Bruges*, published by the Netherlandic Press in Canada in 1983. Some of these had earlier appeared in the English magazines *Ambit* and *Iron*. Peter Nijmeijer's translations were published in two anthologies of the Flemish P.E.N. Centre in Brussels, *Ten Modern Poets from Flanders* (1976) and *Poetry in Flanders Now* (1982), and also in the Scottish magazine *Trends*. Some of my own translations, or their earlier versions, have been published by the magazines *Acumen, Dutch Crossing, The Echo Room, Krino* (Eire), *Ninth Decade, Poesie Europe* (Germany), *The Rialto*. His collected poems *Memoirs: Gedichten 1955–85* was published by Soethoudt (Antwerp, 1985). *Fictieve Winter* was a small press publication, and the poems there were included in his latest collection *Al Wie Omkijkt Is Gezien* (Amsterdam, 1988).

I am especially grateful to Theo Hermans for undertaking at my request some of the more difficult early work, two translations of which were published in the magazine *Folded Sheets*, and for checking my own versions. My thanks also to Willem himself for his unfailing kindness, help and encouragement. Forest Books also wish to thank Pol Mara for allowing us to use his work as illustrations for these poems.

Contents

Translators:
T.H.: Theo Hermans
D.H./H.R.: Dorothy Howard & Hendrika Ruger
Y.L.: Yann Lovelock
P.N.: Peter Nijmeijer
W.R.: Willem M. Roggeman

Introduction

A Painter With Words

Willem M. Roggeman was born in Brussels on 9
July 1935. After study economics at the university
of Ghent, he turned to writing as a career. His
first collection, *Rhapsody in Blue*, appeared when he was 21
and was awarded a prize by the Antwerp literary society De
Nevelvlek in whose journal *Het Kahier* his poems had
originally been published. Other prizes followed, including
the Dirk Martens Prize in 1963, the Louis Paul Boon Prize in
1974, and the literary prize of the city of Brussels for his
collection *Sneeuwblindheid* in 1975. Some dozen books of
poetry have been published, culminating in his collected
poems, *Memoires* (1985), besides two novels written during
the '60s (of which there are French and German translations),
a collection of essays and five of interviews. These last, the
fruit of his work as a journalist, are particularly esteemed
for the insight they give into the work of the artists and
writers concerned. Roggeman was on the staff of the Brussels
daily, *Het Laatste Nieuws*, over the period 1959–81, special-
izing in art and literature; and from 1970 he was one of the
editors of the review *De Vlaamse Gids*. During this time he
was also co-editor of the literary magazine *Kentering*
(Turning-point), 1960–73, and secretary of the Flemish P.E.N.
centre. He moved to Holland in 1981 to become assistant
director of the Flemish Cultural Centre (De Brakke Grond)
and now lives in Hilversum with his francophone wife and
two children. Three selections of his poems in French trans-
lation were published during the '70s and recently one in
German. Another, translated into Macedonian, appeared in
Yugoslavia in 1982, and a Polish selection in 1987. In 1988 the
Belgian government awarded him the Order of Leopold II.

The growth of modernism in Dutch writing has been
characterized by intimate contacts between poets and
painters. Shortly after World War II a modified form of
surrealism began transforming the work of writers and
artists of the 'Generation of the '50s' associated with the
international COBRA movement (largely centred on the

capitals Copenhagen, Brussels and Amsterdam, from the initials of which its name was coined). Several of those in the Belgian capital exhibited their paintings and read their poems at the Taptoe artistic centre, where the young Roggeman first came across them and began to write a poetry of verbal experiment.

Besides sharing the modern aesthetic that the purpose of an art is to demonstrate its own procedures (dating back to the turn of the century), Roggeman was interested in the cross-fertilization of the two arts from the very beginning. He worked together with the painter Maurice Wyckaert on the long poem 'The revolution of the statues'. A later poem, 'The old island and the sea', takes its inspiration from a painting by Wyckaert's friend, Danish Cobra-member Asger Jorn; another deals with Pol Mara, a Belgian abstractionist who turned to Pop Art. The latter has recently repaid the compliment with a watercolour portrait of Roggeman accompanied by one of the artist's characteristic nudes for muse and titled 'Willem's wings' (frontispiece).

It is generally agreed that Roggeman is one of the most painterly of poets, 'a painter with words' as veteran art-critic Paul de Vree called him in an essay of that title. This is to be taken as referring not so much to the use of imagery as to the actual verbal performance. Each word is weighed in a balancing of verbal colours; sentences are deployed with the rhythm of brush-strokes. Not for Roggeman the high flow of rhetoric but short dabs adding up to a general impression. Again, the shape of one of the poems in *Homage to Tinguely* imitates the top-heavy structure of that artist's odd machines. Roggeman shares also, as has already been mentioned, the preoccupation of artists with the nature of reality and the distinction between that and representations in the chosen medium. In 'The eye of the painter' he crosses the line and considers the artist's approach from his idiosyncratic writer's point of view.

Although several of the '50s poets took a radical political stance, they were generally of the opinion that their writing should steer clear of overt propaganda. Their aim was to break down the old structures of form, opinionation, linear thinking and elegant syntax, not to mention anecdotal representation, whereby the literary élite had formerly imposed their conservatism. Revolution should be made in the arts through the arts, as part of a general breaking up of outmoded stances. In the climate of the '60s this came to be viewed as a mandarin attitude in itself and there was a move towards a humanistic commitment such as Jon Silkin was championing in England through his magazine *Stand* and for which stood the Dutch and Belgian editors of *Kentering*, Roggeman among them. 'To a faithful TV watcher' belongs to this period and first appeared in a 1965 anthology. In the course of it he addresses Hans Andreus, a Dutch member of the '50s Experimentalists who was similarly modifying his approach, punning on the title of Andreus' first collection, *Muziek voor kijkdieren.* Such a poem finds its echo in 'High-rise neurosis' and 'For Ulrike Meinhof' over the next decade.

By the end of the '60s the European version of Pop Art known as New Realism (and in Flanders as *De Nieuwe Visie*) was making its impact and again drawing poets and painters together in a common preoccupation. Parisian-based artists like Daniel Spoerri were following the Americans Jasper Johns, Robert Rauschenberg and Tom Wesselman in introducing everyday objects into their work: the shower fixture attached to a landscape in Spoerri's 'Here lies Jean Onnertz' (Galleria Schwarz, Milan), for example. Others like J.F. Arman made assemblages of junk (like the sculpture made of old clocks outside Saint Lazare station in Paris), following the lead of Edward Kienholz in America and the Swiss Tinguely, latter-day disciples of Marcel Duchamp. The influence of Duchamp shows up in Roggeman's 'Ready made' with its built-in quotations and black humour. A similar preoccupation with that artist is to be found in the work of Roggeman's fellow poet and art critic, Roland Jooris, the most talented of the Belgian New Realist writers. During the '70s the work of both probed the nature of artistic and verbal reality in a spare, colloquial style in which play on words is prominent.

Roggeman himself does not fit into any school. He is, rather, a transitional writer (as is suggested by the name 'Turning-point' for the magazine which he co-edited) and demonstrates the characteristics of several. But it is from this time that he comes into his own. His former interest in verbal experiment and alternative structures stood him in good stead now and enabled him to avoid the often limp and vapid artistic chit-chat of the New Realist camp and produce a poetry of suggestiveness and depth. He will only lead us so far; thereafter we must make conceptual leaps of our own in order to keep up with him. Where others drift off into the abstraction of an arid, almost inhuman world, he invariably anchors himself to the human situation. There are times, it must be admitted, when he suffers from a malaise to which our age is particularly prone, a despair which would minimize human value and, on the other extreme, a reactive sentimentality. Luckily Roggeman's sense of humour and eye for telling detail or paradoxical image comes to his rescue most of the time. If everything about reality is doubtful, mere words, then he himself is part of that phenomenon and cannot be taken any more seriously. There is only the play of language, a game in which he joins with gusto.

One might almost say it is as much the way he uses language as anything he says that is Roggeman's strength. His poetry has always been characterized by its verbal ease. At the heart of his mature style lies the contrast between simplicity of diction, even colloquiality, and the way a deceptively plausible syntax either cancels out the sense or leads to treacherous paradox. A house that collapses, as he puts it in one poem, when you knock at its door. Language draws attention to itself in this way, to its power upon our view of reality. Another attention-getter is to pair similar sounding words, a device Roggeman uses for a whole range of effects. An early example appears at the end of one of the stanzas of 'The revolt of the statues', where the word *voorzichtig* (looking ahead, i.e. wary) and *doorzichtig* (see-through, i.e. luminous) are paralleled. Our rendering hardly does it justice. In 'The robot's dream' the phrase 'graceful, gross-fallen' corresponds to Roggeman's *'bevallig, nu bouwvallig'* and strikes a plangent chord. The metronomic variations and repetitions in 'Burgh Sabbath', on the other hand, give exactly the impression of suffocating sameness that the poem describes.

Pun, allusion and buried quotation are other devices of which Roggeman makes frequent use. One of his titles, *Zwijgend in alle dalen*, is based on the idiom 'Silent in all languages' (*talen*), used when someone avoids answering a question (see 'A farewell in Warsaw'). By the change of one letter this modifies to 'Silent in all valleys' – in the context of the poem those feminine declivities and soft hollows to which he makes arch reference elsewhere. 'Silence is bad language' Roggeman suggested in its place, but approved as alternative 'Mum's the word'. In the case of 'A stitch in time', the point of the original title (translating as 'The link between things') and the force of the last line depends on the fact that the Dutch word *verband* means both 'link' and 'bandage'. Roggeman himself rings the changes on a proverb in the final lines of 'Three descriptions of a decrepitude': 'A misfortune never comes alone' is the Dutch variant of our 'Misfortunes never come singly'.

So far as allusion goes, we have already noticed the reference to a title of a book of poems in 'To a faithful TV watcher'. 'Desacrilization' (of the image, the word, the ideas of high art), the stated aim of Dadaists and Surrealists, makes its appearance in 'The old island and the sea', a reference that Asger Jorn might be expected to appreciate as founder-member of a movement strongly influenced by surrealist ideology. Indeed, Roggeman's own desacralization of meaning ultimately stems from the word-games of Duchamp and his fellow thinkers. For example, the sentence *Rose Sélavy et moi esquivons les ecchymoses des Esquimaux aux mots exquis* written round the circumference of a spiralled disc which seems to disappear into itself when rotated in one of the sequences of his *Anemic Cinema*. Language can be manipulated to similar effect, so that it demonstrates no other reality but itself. The pretence that words or paint have any other function is a mere confidence trick. Their true relation to reality is that of the reversed mirror image, a paradox to which Roggeman often returns. 'Realism is the negation of reality' proclaimed one of the COBRA slogans. Or as Roggeman paraphrases, 'Only in language/can I form for myself/a clear picture of reality'.

Roggeman's linguistic stance is that we are victims of verbal conditioning but without it are condemned to an existential and agnostic freedom. It is language that makes things happen, things do not exist in our minds until they are named; language is our only reality. If things change and die, it is because this is the nature of language, the only thing we can know. For him, as for the second century Indian philospher Nagarjuna, even this shadow reality is relative, since words are defined by other words and there is no outside or ultimate reality to which they can be referred. Consequently, quite apart from private understandings and interpretations, any change in one place brings about, because of their interdependence, a shift of meaning throughout the verbal field. There is no firm ground on which to stand. Behind them is the great void (*sunyata*) beyond conceptual expression, a vanishing emptiness.

Being neither philosopher nor mystic, Roggeman can only sport on the borders of such insight, a clown with a riven heart. The suspension of time and space, those anthropomorphic concepts, obviously charms him. Einstein, who helped abolish them, he pictures in retreat before a cackling nature; the discoveries of Columbus are equated with a junkie's visions. As the frozen past melts on encountering the fluid present, the most abstruse of places and people meet in the free medium of the poem. Columbus again, in trying to make sense of the new world of inner space opened to us by the psychologists, can only mouth nonsensical inconsequentialities. Restricted ideas of reality are human fabrications and we only harm others and ourselves by giving any version of it credence, like poor M.M. in 'High-rise neurosis', unhappily isolated in the illusion film has made of her.

Dream, fertile mistress of the Surrealists, is one obvious field of parareality, and Roggeman equates with it the function of poetic language. But he is also sufficiently akin to the Pop Art oriented New Realists to find inspiration in Science Fiction. Edward Lucie-Smith, commenting on the new-style S.F. (or inner space school), remarks that much of it seems to him prose poetry. 'Logic is there, but it is of the kind which we long ago learned to call poetic, meaning by that a way of thinking which moves forward through the use of analogies and hidden correspondencies' – in the way of Roggeman's 'Cosmic poem', for example. Even as the anthology of S.F. poetry, *Holding Your Eight Hands* (the introduction to which is quoted above), first appeared in the U.S. – a British edition followed a year later – Roggeman's obvious candidate for inclusion there, 'Ready, hesitant', was published in his collection *The Oracle of New York*. In the poem he unites the themes of extraterrestrial travel, dream and the figure of the poet, of which 'Poem to be written on a cloud' is a later treatment. The idea of 'A filmed dream', repeated in two poems from *Homage to Tinguely*, also belongs in this area.

The theme of the robot is connected with Roggeman's

distrust of the increasing mechanization of humanity (note for instance the equation of transistors whirring in the grass with 'the coming of the barbarians' in 'Manu militari') and the mechanical models in which man is conceived in 'Ready Made'. This theme also makes its appearance in 'Ready, hesitant' and is allied with that of the mind-made artificial reality in 'A robot's dream'. The title 'The lovesick robot' probably alludes to the same news item referred to in 'The first man on the moon' by the Dutch poet Cees Buddingh', also on the New Realist wing, concerning

> that robot in Denmark
> who said to the journalists
> I don't think it'd be at all a bad thing
> to be a human being.

How that aspiration is possible for human beings themselves, given the constructions of conditioned consciousness that the poem represents, is what troubles Roggeman. If we are the victims of word-made illusions, what is to become of those of them which have given us the little nobility we thought we had, the ideals of love, of human dignity? That the facts belie such ideals is one thing, but that there is no such reality attainable quite another.

For Roggeman, perhaps, it is the fact that such conceptions are possible which is valuable, which restores us our dignity. The answer lies in our creativity. The role of the 'artist' may lead him towards deconstruction, but by his pointing to the process we cease to be the victims of words and are freed: 'each word that you write/makes a breach in the language'. And with this understanding we can build bridges out of our linguistic isolation towards each other.

Yann Lovelock
1988

The Poems

Scene

the village and the night and your breathing
and the silence of your gestures
your legs tearing open
up to the navel
the frenzy of your much too white teeth
my body tense bursting with water
an open door giving onto the dark
there is no measure
to meter your fertility
but
my restive wooden fingers
drumming on your midriff
your voice breaking in a monotone
your hands dimly turning over

desperate the clock hands gaze
a gap in the night

to cleanse oneself with fire
to call oneself drunk
in a glass of water
aware
of being rounded off
of being left behind
to play jazz
with my fingers on your waist
and wait
for the improvisation's end

17 days now
(or centuries) I've wandered
with you as my distant
landing stage

a woman
a house
of flesh and blood
it's comfortable
to dwell there breathing slowly

pinned between her tropics
I deny my organic heritage

in her light brown luminescent blood
dances
the squirrel of my love

Tenir les rênes

because I'm made of air
and aluminium
because I live in clouds
and since she
tastes of greece
because I feed on water plants
and roots

conscience too
walks on stilts
and I lay in her brain
the shining egg of my fear

The revolt of the statues

the drunken mandarin beat the yolk of his black
humour to sneering mayonaise igniting
to a mirror of the sea in which
the drowning man punctiliously played third violin
with a postage stamp over his eyes
and a well-tended little hole in his forehead
like an eccentric in a trance
and clearly reeking with holiness
he wrapped a watch in an incense ashtray
this is the assassin's sweetened pill
he thought chuckling to test himself he shaped
a surly norseman into an aria multicoloured
in the deacon's burning house
and unpolished boots of Pussy without Boots (as old
and blind now as any sparrow) were dancing
and in a fit of lust enlightened despots displayed
the maligned material name of their animal idol
this is space travel a car's derisive cough
this is saintanism a passionate smoker
asleep in a white cloud hence good-humoured equi-
laterally fondling the throbbing bejewelled fur
as the blinking cyclops the king in the country
of the blind who resides in a flame-filled grave
sets out on his long limping quest for the divine substance
the blazing season of
titans playing with parchment erupts like
a poem: a coded miracle play
a prostituted talisman
furious suns light their torches at the dawn
as he flees retching across refuse land
the naive will-o'-the-wisp robbed of its will
by the wind whose hands explore his hands
surfeited with photography
he seeks to give colours a new name
growing fair-haired musical and dissolute
he whirls
colours together
into an explosive painting
so painting is still
running a wary spectacular
a circumspect brilliance

and the disenchanted conjurer
cautiously polishes the brittle dentures of his pets
(their wingbeat spans our lips
their shadow outweighs our silence)

the stalagmite of his nostalgia is as fragrant
as the traffic warden's wig
polyps all around him start softly to breathe
and dogs call to each other the ultimate truth

all the birds are blown apart

he paints an evening leaf on tomorrow's tree
europe's twitching birth
but his ashes turn into defeat in yesterday's mouth
so he stands cold with desire
his hands exploring walls of blue
his face the rubble of a woman's face
and so the dream becomes melancholy blood
slowly tomorrow's roof drifts away
with the corrosive smell of ashes
in desperation he offers you his bloodstained polders
shivering at the frozen borders
of your gleaming silence

the poet is a painted sheep
a sunspectacled cobra a burning limousine
his instrument a screaming steam whistle

this is the last vacant plot of passion
teaching a skull to sing green with despair
and eating the flakes of centuries of adultery
on the delicate stairs
of a cautious house of rain
a lost train of swelling women
the agitations of love in a shivering orchard
the sour chestnut-coloured laughter of heather
as women flee across it on severed fingertips
bloodstained reconciliation of senseless lovers
a deep-sea diver sinking in the wedding
waiting a middle age long for the little shadow-
warrior of my desire to arrive for
poetry is a form of passion
we play down all the organs now
to a whispering spring suite, denying the anger
of the jeering statues

7

Water and blood

The wound hesitates, opens and
cries for knowledge. He whose loving is nameless
dares to go public with his shame.
Years later the landscape
befriends the fugitive.
A memory of tomorrow
rides on lips of mercy.
A star gives itself up.
Impossible, a grenade grows
in my hand, without means,
voiceless, maybe a dream.
The words are made of water and blood.
Soft, the divine roots
of silence,
like an animal's tender handshake,
unlikely as a poetic image.

Sign of life

Now the word's the word.
The poet shuts up in his books
and the word writes itself.
We are all a deaf and dumb generation.
We overcrop the language
without ever coming up with
the meaning of a gesture.
Silence has grown into us
and fear is the screw-
pulled endless fall of a dream.
So everything draws back from coming out.
So everything outgrows us.
The word, barely more than
a sign of life.

Old colonial house

The painted wound

Poetry, open wound.
My flaking shadow.
I start a new stone age.
Damp as a toadstool, my hand
digs ever deeper into the body.
And muddied by daily use my voice
rings chilly in woods dark as a cinema.
Just look, the poem is a place in the country,
light and unreal in summer days.
The word is a translucent raincoat.
In every garage rises the ode to petrol
and in every town the natives kneel
before the oil-god's altar.
Day by day together we reinvent love.
I sleep warm by your body. I want
to practice the matrimonial sport like a science.
The phallic in me will never go under.

Programmatic

Poetry is making visible,
is giving the word a body.
Look, I simply write this down
and I become visible, penetrable.
Poetry is making water fluid,
measuring the fragility of glass,
breathing in a vacuum.
The poem is a solution that is
a mirror image of the riddle.
Hear me when I say:
hollow words need to be filled.
The poem is a statement,
a name for the nameless.

Calligraphic

I hate the word that obliges me
to write it down. The poem
is a struggle with the image,
with the word, with punctuation.
Hence this poem without words.
A surmise, I confirm nothing,
I merely announce that I'm alive,
that perhaps I'm alive,
one day I may know for certain.
Memory remains a boundless white.
Darkness falls around me. To be dead
is to be unconscious for ages.
But already the salt is eating me away.
I am being trodden on.
I am constantly going overboard.

Etymological

The poem is a magnetic field.
The verb lords it in its active form,
word that works and leaves
me out. The word stirs
and grows reverberant in silence and
sunders among the cupboard's china.
Stacked between the softest linen
fragrant in the drawers
the word still breathes. A hand
under sand and cyphers faintly resounds
its letters out of a dead language.
Every time has its limit but
I have outlived myself already.
Every word remains an event.

Graphological

There's the hesitation between words and action
and things still outside the law.
Shall we now deny gravity?
Weighing up the pros and cons
remains a premature pursuit.
In the flowing movement of my writing
that hand goes down for good
and the word is shipwrecked again.
Always arisen inside the shining egg
we develop and become intangible.

On the watercolours of Pol Mara

In the old steepled city of Antwerp
at anchor on the streamlined Scheldt
whose waters saturate the paper
of Pol Mara's aquarelles
water has received its raison d'être.
The slow, running colours combine
into the poetry of an English cottage,
a suburban front garden,
a clear, frosty day in London town.
And in Brussels — mushroom, oilslick —
I now write the silken words
to colour these lines.

He'll never fix a horizon for
it does not belong to this damaged season.
Sometimes an image grows in his eye. He stares
like a man alone in a forest or at sea,
and sneaks a look at the Letters to Milena.
His cries are muffled by the pillow:
these elements of photography.
A pin-up in fine pencil lines
appears between blurred strips of colour.
This is the Renaissance of figuration,
the Appearance of Renovated Man.

No, he will never forget the blood
that appeared like a screaming flower
on President Kennedy's forehead
assassinated in the Dallas streets. The body
suddenly turned into a snow-covered landscape,
the gestures, the movements no longer mattered.

With braided eyes he leans back
in his chair of sand on a lonely dune
and he hears, yes listen, still clearly hears
the soft whir of the wipers
but he's warm and snug in his car,
Shakespeare's sonnets on the back seat,
and rain streams down the windscreen.
You weren't always at ease with it
for movement gets on your nerves,

commotion on the beach, in the water.
It was always like that.
It can still overwhelm you.
A voice was talking on the radio,
an erudite lecture
on white blood cells
or something like that
and you thought of his house
and his two children
and the chill
under his skin.
Joy assumes the taste of a nettle-sting.

This wretched carcass is floating under water now.
You too go under with this unswerving wreck.
You keep repeating the same words
like a woodpecker tapping
at the same trunk.
You see a winking light and you brake a little.
You still hear his words
quiver in your meekness.

Years later you've grown exactly the same,
a frayed sail on the yard
of Re's grave boat,
a rustling underwood of grief.
My words blow back in my face
like November drizzle.

Bolero-Bolero

Manu militari

Monks grin among the greenery,
their feet overset the foundations
of this sanctuary.
But between the lymegrass
the tyrant cautiously steals.

A day assassinated.

Down there behind the greenhouses
the saints still walk
with their dark, cold hate.
Yet amidst ferns and moss
in the early morning
the sun is forgotten.

The general counts his decorations
and then rereads his orders.
Manu militari, i.e. by force of arms
(i.e. with his hand on his heart)
he awaits the coming of the barbarians.

Transistors whir in the grass.

Apathetic

When I sleep
I am timeless and blind
and every dream
passes unseen
in front of my eyes.

The morning is coloured
with the sound of neighbours
exercising their philosophy
a smooth interaction of muscles.

Next the rain is a letter
full of objective memories,
e.g. a bird singing in my breast
or a breathing statue.

All the windows wide open, clawing at the light
and the bankruptcy of every living space.

To wake up is to adjust once more
to the warmth of a body.
To wake up is
to be momentarily immortal.

Immaterial

The day stammers open.
And about what grows in me,
what blows and brews in me,
while all talk glasses
into an exchange of words,
I notice bit by bit:
these are the thousand things
that grow into today.
For what I am
I am wholly.
Look, my words take on life.
Space is filled with strange crops.
Goodwill butters the earth.
But love is a breath
on a mirror
smooth lake.
I still tremble with rage
to my foundations
and grow in her garden
a silver salamander,
a golden snail,
an exceptional mineral.

To a faithful TV watcher

The screen
has enslaved you.
Spring arrives in the city
and you think of
the green meadows and the blue
horses of Franz Marc.
A map of Asia
is flashed before your eyes
and they show you (follow the pointer)
the such and such degree of latitude
which will mark the border
between east and west
but you can't find shelter
from whistling bullets
behind a degree of latitude.
They who invented this landscape
are now secretly hiding in it
at the most you can
polish the rain.
With gold brocade and lace
more precious
than the last breath
of the dying
more precious
than an epitaph
crumbles the space
of this snowy image.
The floor slips away
under your chair and
you have abandoned thoughts.
Oh Hans Andreus
no music
but pictures for mesmerized creatures.
You sit there perplexed
and I ask you now:
Who can match the strength
of this vile weed?

The hollyhock perhaps
on which I wounded myself
around which I wound myself.
Subject closed.

Break the mirror
and see who stands behind it.

The one in paradise

Genesis

Adventure, the word on the move.
The idea turned into a vessel,
form and content are on board.
Sand comes into view behind time.
A theme is brought forth,
pain fully grown into a word,
cultivated into a poem.
I am being spoken.
All my life I inhabit myself,
I carry history inside me
with the tin cup of my tremor
and my hate like a smouldering ruin.
This enlightened thinking. Everything arises
like an Italian Renaissance
out of a hand, a completed gesture.
For hand is movement,
a peninsula, a decorated drought,
a friendship filled with guttural sound.
Symbols glow. But the sun
shrivels in its light.
And time begins.

Ready, hesitant

Shining black and round and
full to bursting as a gasometer,
he rises against the landscape.
And poised for
a moment of overexposure
touches down out of time.
The green toads of his mind
hop up inside the computer,
the robot's oiled brain.

And he says
    In this room
    the web of your words
    hangs motionless yet
or else
    Your eyes are Egypt
    and your hands form
    an inaccessible space.

Like a sea temptation
gleams the soft weed
of sadness in his hair
and the fancied taunt
appears superfluous as moonlight.

The night is only a commentary,
the negative of
the day before.
He knows the whiteness of light
and the fourteen colours of petrol
but through the open window
darkness comes snowing in.
Silence is an inland water,
a wearing down of resistance,
eternity's eating away.
His sleep causes
a short-circuit in time.
The sun's pollen
gleams and morning
unscabs on the horizon.

The lovesick robot

Fear is
a need of words.

The universe is surrounded
with hollow mirrors.
The earth emits
a thousand messages.

The asthmatic monk
paws at the gold-leaf
of mediaeval miniatures
and reads in Bergson's
L'Evolution Créatrice
how the individual consciousness
is being merged
into the collective subconscious.

Somewhere very far away
100 kilometres north of Moscow
Tolstoy's grandson rides
whistling to his work
by motorbike.

Collector's item

The veins of autumn
mutely betoken
the miracle
of leafed gold.

The sea's legible
hand uncovers
yesterday's name
under holy pebbles.

Inland
a sand-filled
skull,
volcanic treasure.

Nightwood,
decoded silence,
trees screaming
from every leaf.

Frieeze

The eyes
blink
a moment
at the morning walls.

Then mark
how light fingers
glass green
in the room.

Behind barred words
breath steals
out and back,
out and back.

Clouds
break alight.

A train going to my dreams

Eulogy of the metaphor

Blindfold, love flees
on an oldfashioned bicycle
(you know, one with a very
big and a very small wheel)
over the wash
of a husky high summer.

The beauty queen
walks on subjective stilts
and the other contestants
flop in her fairway,
upon which fallen leaves
shudder.

The sun winks
but otherwise keeps its thoughts to itself.

And man,
he lives cautiously,
his nails retracted,
his rustling
proves short-lived.

High-rise neurosis

In a tenth-floor apartment
near noon wakes the film star M.M.
to cross in a see-through
negligé and bare foot
over soft carpets
for a silent moment
eye to eye with herself
in the mirror and think:

Here I stand, then,
poplar-slim, popular.

Down at mouth,
she murmurs:

But in my body
I am the only passenger.

Then she begins the day
with orange-juice,
not knowing whether
gin or whiskey will
end it.

A filmed dream

Unpunished
a poet plays havoc
with the language,
sets the use of words
on loose screws.
In his hand
he has the key
of a world
that breathes in and out
and looks with washed eyes
across this potato field.
His camera-eye
plays Peeping Tom with
the blind sexuality
of human and human
until he becomes lyrical.
A life in the service
of writing, of
the movement of a hand.
This is becoming
too crazy.

Reap the night

Sometimes I take the shape
of a human being.

Then I indulge myself
in all that is human.

Then I create poetry and say
yearning things such as:

Shall I compare thee
to a summer day as
Shakespeare has done?

A day suffuses me.
Morning fog colours the city colourless,
the house withdraws its shelter.
Sunday: a day without sin.

In the silence of the morning
the sun keeps itself deathly quiet.
Sometimes in a dream I hear
the falling of earth on me.

A feminine presence
becomes thin and imaginary.
Only the silver of her breath . . .

Love remains an infamous occupation,
a rhythmic doom.
Softened by the moisture
of an eye
I get the impression of passion.

Thus I am destroyed.
Reaching out to touch.
With a sound of pain
inside.
With a feeling that something
of me dies.
And with nothing to be thankful for,
evidently.

Love poem

I know you will die
as beautiful as ever.
With a smile
round your lips e.g.
or with a flower in your hand.
And in subsequent days
the dust will lie somewhat thicker
on the window-sill.
It'll be very nice weather.
Nice and hard blue.
I shall walk about
with strange thoughts
and my head
still deeper between my shoulders.
Then a word of consolation
will come from someone
least expected.
And for the rest
everything will remain
as it was.

For a lonely day

That's how it goes (sometimes)

The sun is rising too late
and then plays between the trees
but keeps itself safe
at the edge of the world.
Through the wall intrudes
the television of neighbours
spreading melancholia.
The poet tells lies
in thin little books
and imagines himself a Gulliver
in the depth of his thoughts.
And a rare reader
trusts him at his word.
Outside the last landscape
is being covered with concrete.

The old island and the sea

(from a painting by Asger Jorn)

The word swims in the poem
like an old island
in the sea. And the sun?
It descends shyly, going ahead
of its light, showers of sorrow
between shadows of love.
You and I fall in company
and are polluted with poetry.
The rain is of short order.
A shabby shame
lords over marble centuries
that sink by degrees
to this stammering statue.
With a ritual brushstroke
Asger Jorn passes
to the desacralization
of religion.
Of what dream
is he the author?
Nothing is left him
but supposition.
He knows that feeling.
He goes outside
the limits of time.

Poem with big words

Doubt hesitates in me.
You want to feel my words
with wary fingers.
The rick gives off its scent. And love
is body to body combat
you say. An old saying:
words come to grips.
Breathing in a fragment of time,
of what I rank below belief,
you grow slowly
from your name.
An eagle is netted
in the light's necklace.
Remembrance is a hollow
that lives in the hollow
of a memory.

Ready made

A sun of neon rises.
How does it feel to live
in this era
of rapid changes
and boundless information
or pseudo-information
via the image?
According to Kudo
Hiroshima was not exceptional,
sooner characteristic
for whatever it is,
for instance for
what happens here and now.
He considers life
from a distance,
as an interesting
though senseless process.
You can breed it
through radio activity
in an electric circuit.
Sex is nothing but
such a process.

On a crisp morning

Between the grass of this landscape
I place words like
tree, cow and
afternoon sun.
Heartwarming
is this last,
just like a poem
that I save
jealously
as a remembrance
for later,
for much later.

Déjeuner sur l'herbe

Written in gothic

Hölderlin cries in his hammock.
A button is missing
from his silver dressing-gown.
Nobody is ever born again
he thinks full of homesickness
for the grass of Greenland.
From his tower
he has a beautiful view
but in his room
with the olive green walls
he places his bare feet
time and again
in his own footsteps.
And at his desk
in his beautiful gothic handwriting
he jots down:
when I collect
your moments of silence
I clearly notice
your eloquence.

Mum's the word

Sometimes I feel caught
when she gives me the
eye when you know when.
Then I tell her:
this poem
is written on your body.
The words are well
matched. It's all a question
of living and outliving
for death is a collective noun,
an underground station, a rest-cure,
but all the same safer
than this rosy trap,
your finger in the timetable.
That clinches it.

Poem to recopy

1.

Woman of wounds and mouths,
once you outdid routine
for beauty.
You were quiet
as the course of a sad journey's length
and I treasured you
as I did my death
and the seed of pinetrees.
Woman with the thousand lips
who danced with loud laughing body
on the clifftop of your fear
until you tipped backward
into the night.
You are a new beginning.

2.

A new beginning you are.
You treasure your sadness
for you live slower then.
Time withers to
the gliding by of clouds
the sound of rain falling
wanting to know no one any more
wanting to know no more of anyone.
You are a still-life,
a single rose in a little water.
You are
a book that falls
and remains lying open
while the wind
plays among the pages.

From my document case

Long ago Columbus
set foot on shore here;
wet finger lifted in the wind,
he triumphantly recorded
periwinkles and pertussus.
Posing for the photographers,
one foot on a dead indian,
he tells the press later:
here man is
a strange mineral,
rare as a weed
or a brand-new giant.
In his flesh and blood
plant nature still stirs.
The Stone Age
comes to life in his brain
and only in winter
is his breath visible.
On his retina
spots and lines merge
to form an anonymous picture,
a mirror of the cosmos.

Three descriptions of a decrepitude

1. It's a rotten truth
    that life is a sickness
    to which you've sooner or later
    got to give up the ghost.
    And meanwhile each happy chance
    stands me in stead.
    What is it happens
    to language that under my hand
    unresistingly line after line
    subjects itself to new rules?
    So I defend myself softly
    against homesickness and sorrow.

2. In this convoy of words
    hides my call, my ruse,
    the noose that rings you in.
    Your body grows transparent.
    My glance bores through the light of your years
    and don't I see your flesh grow softer?
    Only when I'm silent
    do you understand me fully.
    And though unseizable
    I'm not my shadow either
    and my reflection stays
    a stranger to me always.

3. I have written myself off
    from my own account.
    With the blackest hope
    I laugh defiantly
    in the fading landscape.
    Then I wait and know
    how imagination rises
    out of contradiction and
    what I choose to be going on with
    or curse under my breath.
    Misfortunes always come
    when you're alone.

Zondag in de stad

Leeg, dan leger,
dan lager raakt
het bewustzijn jou.

Je handen bergen
bergen herinneringen.
Het huis luistert
naar zijn grijze muren als
naar een Duits wiegelied.

Zo is de stad
een onleesbaar verhaal
van stenen op stenen
op stenen.

Burgh Sabbath

Toom, then louch,
then laich, ca's
your kenning to you.

Your han's sort
orts o memorie.
The biggin gies lug
to its lyart wa's as gin
to an Alleman bairney sang.

So the toun turns
an abradit tale
o stanes on stanes
on stanes.

The robot's dream

Every day we make
reality up.
Still this stays true,
daddy's strong, mummy's nice
and happiness is a toy train
left behind in the nursery.
This picture I focus poetically
with memory's spectacles.
I feel my shadow take flight
and know the mouth that will name me
in a still softer hollow.
The evening is wrapped in cellophane.
So I look
at your once graceful, gross-fallen
body. Silence is a word
that nowhere echoes back.
Whenever you open your eyes
the world is remade.

Poem to be written on a cloud

Between burning snow and melting stones,
between glowing ice and steamy clouds,
he leads an extraterrestrial existence.
Hanging from the parachute of his words
he descends into the depths of time.

He walks singing among the strange plants
of an unknown planet.
And when the light begins to change
he's filled with what he never felt.

Long ago he started
rubbing out our memories.
A thinking being, he says,
will never add up to more
than a little electric.
The cosmos is my reflection,
the void my self-portrait.

Through the window he sees
glassy-eyed
how a landscape forms hesitantly
out of grass and trees and a bit of cool clay.
No need to go on:
each glance creates an optical illusion.

Divina ballerina

Season to season

Time hangs fire in the mirror.
Sunlight lights me up
and endlessly swings on
season to season
as if from branch to branch
in a forest of years
yet progressing
with the swiftness of imagination.
Sometimes a word leaps
beyond language
and turns into a star,
then a cinder.
Always after each sun
inevitably follows the blinding.
What does always mean?
The length of a summer's day
in the scorched countryside.
The cracked mirror image
of twin brothers.
What won't pass:
the warmed silence
gathered in her mouth.
Yesterday's cooled ashes.
What's left me?
A prospect of words.

Columbus in New York

When Columbus discovered America
he couldn't believe his eyes.
He'd come with his shipmates
in search of a guru
and really set his sights on India.
But as his ship the Santa Maria
was on the point of sinking he was picked up
by the harbour police and sailed
past the Statue of Liberty and a bit later
was craning up among the skyscrapers.
I'll have to tell my queen about this, he thought.
Who'd have expected skyscrapers in India?
Next morning his picture was splashed across
the front page of the *New York Herald Tribune*
and shares in Indian hemp
rocketed on Wall Street.
In a sleezy dive in the Bowery
Columbus gave himself a fix
and in a whirling of colours
imagined himself commander
of a fifteenth century Spanish caravel.

Unchanged, but unrecognizable

By the sea, he says, by the sea it's all different,
everything there is stir and sough. There you live
with the smell and the smack of salt on lip.
For that's what the sea's like, beautiful as a lie.
But something in reality keeps slipping back.
Was it here that you found love, she asks.
His answer is no answer.
Sadness grates between his teeth
as if he'd sucked sandgrains in.
Close by the beach gulls fly over the sea.
Sometimes it looks like they're touching
the foam of the waves with their wings.
Look, he says, white against white. Like then and now.
He's talking to her. Wiping his eye.
Secretly at a tear.
There's something in my eye, he fibs.
Her words cut like splinters of the past.
His recollections haver in
the middle ages of his life.
Inside his mouth her words feel
warm and moist. Blood? he thinks.

The colours of dream

Last night I awakened with the irritating question:
Do all colours occur in dreams?
Or, to phrase the question another way:
Can anyone dreaming see a rainbow completely?
Orange is there for sure. Just look at the oranges
glowing softly in the bright yellow bowl.
There is also the red of the setting sun
and the purple of deep shadows.
There is green of meadows and plants
and especially much grey,
of walls, of water, often of the sky.
And after a long hot summer, much brown.
But blue, no, that's not there.
Blue is the colour of waking
when you are bent over me
and I look straight into the deep blue of your eyes.

Life is like a movie,
your true colours show

Summer was very erotic again.
With short skirts and
low-cut décolletés.
So once more we felt younger
than we were.
In those days our happiness
was still as good as new.
We closed our eyes
the better to listen
to the sounds of the past.
The vagueness of our memories
made us doubt
if we'd lived to the fullest.
For life whirls by like a film.
You understand it only at the end.
And each time it's the same,
when you tell me
everything's all right
and kiss me long and warm
behind shut eyes
I see spelled out THE END.

And the kitchen became woman

Einstein discovers autumn

Also he collects the gold dust
of fallen leaves in the park when autumn comes.
Then clouds begin to hang very low
as if pushed down by curiosity.

He sees a giant hand
lies protectively across the hill.
And under a glass cupola
rain and wind rage silently.

Finally, close to exhaustion,
the old man shuts the window,
locking out the last morning
while the sun scrupulously begins hiding
within the foliage
and the grass furtively screeches
with scarcely suppressed joy.

The revolution begins in Bruges

In this city everyone reads
with almost mediaeval patience
the manuscript of water.
Morning breaks the sun open
and someone arranges flowers of glass.
Sunlight falls like a stream
on untidy and still warm sheets.
Someone enters the room
as if he stepped off the world.
She still walks wrapped in colours of sleep.
On her eyelashes hang drops of light.
Someone mentions a name: Hans Memling
and someone else points questioningly at himself.
Someone runs fast in the park.
In the trees rustles a girl's name.
Someone returns from nowhere
his travel memories forgotten.
The city sings in all its kiosks,
in closed movie theatres and restaurants
dream images and appetite hangs heavy.
Neon signs stand black and useless,
their symbols are words no longer.
Someone accepts the facts,
someone else waits for a sign
and a third looks up rapt.
Whose rapier has run the clouds through?

The poet has no excuse

Surprised by reality,
the world becomes your second residence,
but basically you belong in this text.
For all refers back to all:
the house to its inhabitant
the poem to its maker,
the air to who breathes it.
And friendship is only a word
among many others. Just as silence,
so I presume,
is also a form of sound.
For as things were, so they become.
Never alone, but always solitary.
So your voice has quietly gone
brown as autumn.
Over the years
a man grows
more and more uninhabitable.
But the poet has no excuse
for growing older
for he always holds some poem
in reserve.
And each word that you write
makes a breach in the language.

A primary presentiment

The man down on his knees
crackles like paper.
On the windows of my bedroom
my dreams are painted
— e.g. a white horse
on a dark blue background
and springing up everywhere the avid grass
of my notes in the margin.
The days cross my body
to which sleep clings each morning.
The wind blows through my bones.
You are a dismantled city
I hear said in a daydream.
But each experience of the future
flows over our faces like kindness.
A frightened look in the mirror
and today is growing blurred already.
Meanwhile everything proves I was
on my way to birth for generations.

Looking and seeing

I'm on my way to language.
Glancing through the window
I see reality
— my reality, that is:
a bit of the garden, a pond,
a street bordered by villas.
A minuscule portion
of a limitless reality.
A part, furthermore,
I've observed very poorly.
For now my attention
comes back to this paper
I really can't remember
whether the sun was dazzling
or just dim.
When I write, I'm certain again.
Only in language
can I form for myself
a clear picture of reality.

Parlez à mezzo-voce

The birth of a myth

A bird that isn't
becomes a red word
burning in language's black.
I carry its name in me
like a scar of braille.
Continually suspect
but clean as a knife-edge
I admit I adopt
a recognisable shape.
I am a lonely shore
that awaits for years
the unrolling
of the first wave.
So I unword,
a speech without masks,
not to be misunderstood.
The south bears my palm off.
The sun blusters
on the horizon
but I remain hostage
to this land
on which I stand like a plumbline.
One by one I make the words up.

Meanwhile something else is always going on

When I say something
it always comes out different
from what I meant.
The words, yes,
they're easy to grasp.
But they come over, come
through the lips, with such difficulty.
I don't need to
hold out my hands
to know the softness
of rain falling
on dewy grass or moss
or something else
equally tender,
for example your cheek.
And when I try to say it,
naturally in other words,
then she looks at me
kindly like a stranger.
She is my returning dream
that brings almost
the shock you feel
when the house collapses
after you've just been knocking at the door.

Poem for Ulrike Meinhof

Some can't take any more.
Some paint a mirror on the wall
with the face of a woman in it.
Some listen to a tape
with the voice of a woman
whose whispering can hardly be heard.
Some feed their imagination
with recollections of adventures
they never experienced.
Some see in the creases
of the blanket on the bed
the shape of a sleeping woman.
Some fall asleep
with one hand in the hand of the night.
Some whisper I love you
and listen to the stove's answer.
Some can't agree with themselves.
Some know the precise personal description
of a woman they never knew.
Some point to the place
where alcohol gave birth to beauty.
Some sit motionless in a room
and travel with dizzying speed
through the country that begins behind the mirror.
Some are afraid of the sunrise.
Some answer the questions
that no-one ever asked them
due to lack of interest.
Some see in the wallpaper
how life passes by.
Some can't even talk to themselves.
Some don't realize that yesterday has never begun.
Some sink like stones into time.
Some feel their blood stop running.
No one is alone in his loneliness.

Feeding the hungry

Because the moon slowly becomes edible
as the night draws to an end.

Because someone stole a strip of sunlight
from the store cupboard
and with infected hands
put his hunger in its place.

That's why the village constable dreams
of being in dress uniform and eloquent.

Invulnerable in his shirtsleeves
he struts onto the stage
behind his overfed belly.
His courage beams forth from his helmet.

He has the law on his side for
he licks upward and kicks downward.
But with his leather boots on, invested
with authority and power, he occasionally throws
a shining white bone to the faint ones below.

For those who've gone hungry for so long
that you can count their ribs
through transparent skin
love to wallow in the dust
even if it's for a mere bone.

Even as the night bulges with silence
you can hear the homely sound of their gnawing.

The painter's eye

The landscape lies stiffened
under a thin coat of varnish.

What is reality, then?
The chaotic version of what
the painter has ordered.

In this still-life he looks
in vain for a human being,
finds only a small pile of clothes
in a corner of the studio.
For where life stands still
the model soon grows tired.
And after hours of naked immobility
her lips have a taste of raspberries.

On the mirror he paints
his self-portrait
over his reflection.

At brown finger-ends he grips
a cigarette on which he draws thoughtfully
then blows the smoke out slowly,
creating about the mirror a halo
furrowed with blue waverings.

I paint my portrait,
therefore I am, he says philosophically.

All is stilled within the picture, falls
silent within the eye's compass.

The painter mixes colour on his palette
and endows the world with his perspective.
With the stem of his brush
he measures planes.
The air weighs heavily on the earth.

He fills up with dabs of colour
all the blanks in the world.
He opens a window and

rain starts falling hard
inside the house
while outside the sun shines.

The wall splits and reveals
the continual variations of the light.

The room slides back together.
The world also. Marrying the dimensions
of the painting.

Yes, but what does it represent?
The picture has no other
subject than itself.
What is portrayed there
was pictured for years
in the painter's eye.
It only remains to
imagine reality.

A Farewell to Warsaw

Inside my head green predominates.
A large park grows there with many trees
and in the centre a statue of Chopin
and many benches where in summer
you can listen to his music in the blazing sun.

Inside my head ochre predominates.
The colour of the old market and of
the royal palace, the colour that
gives Warsaw the taste of saffron.
In this city melancholy
is written with rain on the windowpanes.
He who lives here knows how darkness grows
on the other side of the window.
And the reflection of the lamp
in the black glass more and more resembles
an image of loneliness.

A psychiatrist enters my field of vision
and explains the dreams of the
melancholy sales-ladies in large department stores.
In the meantime a poet suffers poverty
between his piles of manuscripts.

Inside my head brown predominates.
The colour of your eyes when you
look at me a long time and are silent in all tongues.
Stars pasted on the firmament
of a dream landscape.
Winter and snow on the windscreen wipers.
Somebody stupidly walks into a tram.
The last face he saw
lies frozen in his eyes.

Portrait of a painter's dog

Cosmic poem

When after years this poem
goes up with a bang
because the inner stress
has grown too great
then the words will
keep pulsing further apart
and each of them lead
its own separate existence,
so that their meaning also
becomes subject to change in its turn.
(For words are like people,
their meaning
depends on each other.)
Perhaps some smaller words will
turn in orbit then round another word
that has a greater attraction
because it consists of more letters.
In that case the word sun
won't be the centre of this Milky Way of speech
but only a satellite
of for example the word starshimmer.

Archaeological find

Recently an archaeologist
committed a terrible blunder.
He unearthed from the sands
in the Nevada desert
the radioactive remains
of a roulette wheel,
thus proving beyond question
that Las Vegas really existed.
Manifestly the poor devil
had been digging in the wrong direction
and in a manner stumbled
on the last vestiges of our future.

Poem with built-in silence

I'd like to be able to write like this.
The way the sun sparkles in the glass
and the warm wine shines
on the white table in the garden.
Or the way you saunter round a museum
and whisper: that picture,
I'd like to own it,
it would look good in the living-room,
I'd gaze at it every day
and never grow tired of it.
And you think, astonished:
this is a declaration of love.
But you know love never
turns out how you thought it would.
You look at your hands and think:
whom will they still caress
before they grow old and wrinkled?
But you know: with no one else
can you be silent as with her.
And you smile because the taste is there again.
You sample a small slice of the sun
that slowly melts on your tongue.

Goya's black

Give me a piece of charcoal
and I draw a picture,
he said.

He had twenty children of whom
only one would survive him.

As court painter at Aranjuez he painted
Charles IV's family standing
and made a separate study of each figure.
The king he presented with
his *Los Caprichos* sketchbook
in order to avoid the Inquisition.

Everything's a lie
and all women deceivers.

And who was it again had to die
because he'd discovered the earth rotates?
Who will ever heal
this mutilation of the truth?

War has nothing to do
with heroism, he says in
Los Desastres de la Guerra.
In that Dantesque underworld
men are condemned
to become shadows.

Acid bites into copper
black images of the struggle
between reason and the dream of reason,
between darkness's seething
and the logic of light.

He painted the Duchess of Alba
in a black mantilla
and with a red sash round her waist.
Red was her favourite colour.

Like all Spanish women of the time
the duchess was vain, of no great intelligence
and without culture, but her beauty
and her pride made her bewitching.

She was the greatest passion
in his life.

In 1792 he had an apoplexy
which left him deaf.
He only understood
a primitive dumbshow.

Fibrous as rape, her voice,
but he had stopped hearing.
Fiery as an ape, the voice
that his deafness hushed.
His ears stayed closed
to those who had nothing to say.
But his wakeful eye fixed on
throne and altar, tyranny and lies,
contempt for the people and
the outcasts' miseries.

Their love came deft to his deafness.
And she died when she turned forty.

In the deafman's house
he painted on the walls
fourteen black pictures
of abominable scenes like
"Saturn devouring one of his children".
He found here a demonic pleasure.

Where do you discover lines in nature?
Black stains eat into everything.

For the sake of his rheumatism
he left for Bordeaux.
There he would die, a voluntary exile.
The duel between black and white
was at an end.

La mangeuse de masques

Homage to Tinguely

1. Machine for exploring things passed

It starts like a statue turning round
to see what distance it
has covered all these years.
Like the sighs of a bed
that for years on end has known love
and is empty now. Like a mad
metronome that keeps ticking faster.
Like the smear of words on a pillow.
Like the look of old men in portraits
of centuries ago that hang
in dark corridors where
people pass no longer.
They know the secret.
The older you get, the
slower you live. Or is there
something out of true in time?
She looks at me as if
I was still about.
Time escapes
her. Just look,
I'm not there at
all any more,
I'm not
even
here.

2. Machine that works on the power of imagination

Whoever dreams near this strange machine
will set it unknowingly in motion
and notice how it wraps the world
in the rags of his imagination.
Its screw turns much faster
than a flash of thought.
It greedily sucks up all sounds
and makes out of them silence.
Mechanically the oceans
are apportioned. Without noise it produces
prefabricated castles in air.
All that arises here
exists for the first time.
It is also an outstanding
conductor of the dead.
For those who don't believe
there follows a description
of the beyond, recorded
with the utmost accuracy
like the inventory of
vacuum.

3. Machine to make dreams visible

You stand waiting at a bus-stop
but a hearse draws up in front of you.
A snow-white hand beckons
inviting you in.
But your leaden limbs won't budge.
Your quivering eyelids betray the story
that unrolls behind your forehead.
Electrodes are fixed to your temples.
The authorities keep watch day and night
over your mental health
and have made this machine compulsory.
So it's under control how you
build untranslatable forms
out of a scaffold of mist.
Spectres grow like mildew
over the screen. Someone talks
but stays out of the picture.
A woman's face, your mother's at 30,
becomes the girl you saw yesterday
on a hoarding for toothpaste.
It's a wonder
the glass crystals aren't smashed
when you burst out laughing like that.
You hear again the dialect
of your childhood. People
appear against a village
background. Trees
inexplicably blossom. From their branches
fall the first
dewdrops of morning.

4. Machine for pumping the sadness out of people

This is a merry mobile,
rattling and thumping,
piercing and shaking,
sucking speech out of the cylinder
of the subconscious.

But a waterproof sadness
takes digging the heels in.

Standing still between scrap on the go
this machine keeps on lustily pumping,
whirring and grinding,
panting and thumping,
the sadness out of people.

I'm clear of the clouds
right now, says someone.
What is nameless becomes visible.

5. Machine that makes the world go round

The harder it turns, the more beautiful
the world becomes. A blue planet
that sometimes spills a little life over the edges.
Glass clouds tap one against the other.

Always in the same rhythm
this machine turns towards the future.
Time sucks everything in.

Nothing is so fragile as silence,
so light of colour and nevertheless
so heavy to bear.

The sun and the moon are ready
to sink into their own footprints.
The evening clouds are of water
and wash; they look like a painting.

The world throws its shadow off,
it falls on nothing.
A vanishing emptiness.

Linten-legende

God's dream

If it's true that we're
all only characters
peopling God's great
endless dream, then he's also
dreaming all our dreams and has no
power to interfere in our existence
since he's not conscious of it.
That he's invented in his dream
Shakespeare as much as Eichmann
testifies to his fantastic imagination.
When the time comes for him
to wake from this nightmare, perhaps he'll
create some divine Freud
who will analyse this dream
and explain it. Then will appear
from what complexes God suffers.
In the future then we shall
likely experience a calmer existence,
but if the therapy miscarries
we're in for stranger
stories yet.

A stitch in time

When it was there, it didn't exist.
Now it's there no longer
it exists more than ever before.
What I remove from the landscape
grows irrevocably part of me.
It's as if I snip a small piece out of time
and keep it a moment.
Memory's like that too.
Something that's been cut
out of a much larger whole.
Only the gap can still
clearly be seen.
It's like a very old wound.
Only the stitches remain.

Resonance of time

Hail in July, fictive winter.
An iron scale that breaks,
repetition of a favourite gesture.
Like water in spate sometimes
ing-land resembles an island.
Memory bursts open.
A stain on the plain.

Today was late
for its engagement.
Shrapnel of words
on language's battle-field.
Who tells tales there
against nature?
A blinding dialogue
of leitmotiv and lightning.

The plain flows out,
silence of endless days.
Not a stone stirs.
Nothing occurs there.

He who looks back is lost

Just as if what he sees
were visible indeed.

Wherever sea touches land
the curtain of seeming is torn.

All he never wanted to know
he let slip again slowly.

The dream became a row of images
so that the sound cut.

In the becalmed zone
of his imagination
he inhabits an uninhabited island.

Memory eructs in the room.

This is like a new copy
of a year long gone.

So he also has vanished.
Somewhere he opened a door,
stepped into a house full of light,
the squat of her heart.

Where he once was
it's emptier than ever now.

Counting the scores up

Winter requires much patience.
Abiding the tide's
turn till ice unhardens. Viewing
along hedgerow and garden
the movement of the moon.
Pounding both ears flat the farmer
hears how the house shivers in the night,
how his dreams thaw crackling
under the electric blanket.

The landscape lies tucked
in a bit of old sun.

His memories tumble
tinkling within him
like an icecube falling
to the bottom of a glass.

Watching how a wall cracks,
how a seagull glides over the ice,
white as a shriek.

All white. All scored out.

Other Titles from
FOREST BOOKS

Special Collection

THE NAKED MACHINE Selected poems of Matthías Johannessen.
Translated from the *Icelandic* by Marshall Brement.
(Forest/Almenna bokáfélagid)
0 948259 44 2 cloth £7.95   0 948259 43 4 paper £5.95   96 pages
Illustrated

ON THE CUTTING EDGE Selected poems of Justo Jorge Padrón.
Translated from the *Spanish* by Louis Bourne.
0 948259 42 6 paper £7.95   176 pages

ROOM WITHOUT WALLS Selected poems of Bo Carpelan.
Translated from the *Swedish* by Anne Born.
0 948259 08 6 paper £6.95   144 pages. Illustrated

CALL YOURSELF ALIVE? The love poems of Nina Cassian.
Translated from the *Romanian* by Andrea Deletant and
Brenda Walker. Introduction by Fleur Adcock.
0 948259 38 8 paper £5.95.   96 pages

RUNNING TO THE SHROUDS Six sea stories of Konstantin
Stanyukovich. Translated from the *Russian* by Neil Parsons.
0 948259 06 X paper £5.95   112 pages. Illustrated

PORTRAIT OF THE ARTIST AS AN ABOMINABLE SNOWMAN
Selected poems of Gabriel Rossenstock translated from the
Irish by Michael Hartnett. New Poems translated by Jason Sommer.
Dual text with cassette.
0 948259 56 6 paper £7.95   112 pages

LAND AND PEACE Selected poems of Desmond Egan translated
into Irish by Michael Hartnett. Gabriel Rossenstock, Douglas
Sealey and Tomas MacSiomoin. Dual text.
0 948259 64 7 paper £7.95   112 pages

THE EYE IN THE MIRROR Selected poems of Takis Varvitsiotis.
Translated from the *Greek* by Kimon Friar. (Forest/Paratiritis)
0 948259 59 0 paper £8.95   160 pages

THE WORLD AS IF Selected poems of Uffe Harder.
Translated from the *Danish* by John F. Deane and Uffe Harder.
0 948259 76 0 paper £4.95   80 pages

THE TWELFTH MAN Selected poems of Iftighar Arif.
Translated from the *Urdu* by Brenda Walker and Iftighar Arif.
Dual text.
0 948259 49 3 paper £6.95   96 pages

SPRINGTIDES Selected poems of Pia Tafdrup.
Translated from the *Danish* by Anne Born.
0 948259 55 8 paper £6.95   96 pages

Snow and Summers Selected poems of Solveig von Schoultz. Translated from *Finland/Swedish* by Anne Born. Introduction by Bo Carpelan. Arts Council funded.
0 948259 52 3 paper £7.95   128 pages

Heartwork Stories of Solveig von Schoultz. Translated from *Finland/Swedish* by Marlaine Delargy and Joan Tate. Introduction by Bo Carpelan.
0 948259 50 7 paper £7.95   128 pages

Thickhead and Other Stories Stories by Haldun Taner. Translated from the *Turkish* by Geoffrey Lewis. unesco collection of representative works.
0 948259 59 0 paper £8.95   176 pages

East European Series

Footprints of the Wind Selected poems of Mateja Matevski. Translated from the *Macedonian* by Ewald Osers. Introduction by Robin Skelton. Arts Council funded.
0 948259 41 8 paper £6.95   96 pages. Illustrated

Ariadne's Thread An anthology of contemporary Polish women poets. Translated from the *Polish* by Susan Bassnett and Piotr Kuhiwczak. unesco collection of representative works.
0 948259 45 0 paper £6.95   96 pages

Poets of Bulgaria An anthology of contemporary Bulgarian poets. Edited by William Meredith. Introduction by Alan Brownjohn.
0 948259 39 6 paper £6.95   112 pages

Fires of the Sunflower Selected poems by Ivan Davidkov. Translated from the *Bulgarian* by Ewald Osers.
0 948259 48 5 paper £6.95   96 pages. Illustrated

Stolen Fire Selected poems by Lyubomir Levchev. Translated from the *Bulgarian* by Ewald Osers. Introduction by John Balaban. unesco collection of representative works.
0 948259 04 3 paper £5.95   112 pages. Illustrated

An Anthology of Contemporary Romanian Poetry Translated by Andrea Deletant and Brenda Walker.
0 9509487 4 8 paper £5.00   112 pages.

Gates of the Moment Selected poems of Ion Stoica. Translated from the *Romanian* by Brenda Walker and Andrea Deletant. Dual text with cassette.
0 9509487 0 5 paper £5.00   126 pages
Cassette £3.50 plus VAT

SILENT VOICES An anthology of contemporary Romanian women poets. Translated by Andrea Deletant and Brenda Walker.
0 948259 03 5 paper £6.95   172 pages.

EXILE ON A PEPPERCORN Selected poems of Mircea Dinescu. Translated from the *Romanian* by Andrea Deletant and Brenda Walker.
0 948259 00 0 paper £5.95   96 pages. Illustrated

LET'S TALK ABOUT THE WEATHER Selected poems of Marin Sorescu. Translated from the *Romanian* by Andrea Deletant and Brenda Walker.
0 9509487 8 0 papger £5.95   96 pages.

THE THIRST OF THE SALT MOUNTAIN Three plays by Marin Sorescu (Jonah, The Verger, and the Matrix). Translated from the *Romanian* by Andrea Deletant and Brenda Walker.
0 9509487 5 6 paper £6.95   124 pages. Illustrated

VLAD DRACULA THE IMPALER A play by Marin Sorescu. Translated from the *Romanian* by Dennis Deletant.
0 948259 07 8 paper £6.95   112 pages. Illustrated

THE ROAD TO FREEDOM Poems and Prose Poems by Geo Milev. Translated from the *Bulgarian* by Ewald Osers. UNESCO collection of representative works.
0 948259 40 X paper £6.95   96 pages

IN CELEBRATION OF MIHAI EMINESCU Selected poems and extracts translated from the *Romanian* by Brenda Walker and Horia Florian Popescu. Illustrated by Sabin Balaşa.
0 948259 62 0 cloth £14.95   0 948259 63 9 paper £10.95   224 pages

THROUGH THE NEEDLE'S EYE Selected poems of Ion Miloş. Translated from the *Romanian* by Brenda Walker and Ion Miloş.
0 948259 61 2 paper £6.95   96 pages. Illustrated

YOUTH WITHOUT YOUTH and other Novellas by Mircea Eliade. Edited and with an introduction by Matei Calinescu. Translated from the *Romanian* by MacLinscott Ricketts.
0 948259 74 4 paper £12.95   328 pages

A WOMAN'S HEART Stories by Jordan Yovkov. Translated from the *Bulgarian* by John Burnip.
0 948259 54 X paper £9.95   208 pages

Fun Series

JOUSTS OF APHRODITE Poems collected from the Greek Anthology Book V. Translated from the *Greek* into modern English by Michael Kelly.
0 948259 05 1 cloth £6.95   0 94825 34 5 paper £4.95
96 pages